'AMONG THE GIANTS'

Student Workbook and Journal

By Jesse LeBeau & Donee Bilderback-LeBeau

HOW TO BEGIN THIS PROGRAM

-FIRST; MAKE SURE YOU HAVE READ, "AMONG THE GIANTS". Feel free to use the book as a textbook. Write notes to yourself in it, underline the passages that speak to you the most, and jot down questions or concerns you have as you are reading.

-SECOND; READ THE WORKBOOK INTRODUCTION AND TAKE THE ONLINE ASSESSMENT I MENTION IN THE TABLE OF CONTENTS (and in life lesson #11). This will help you identify some of your interests and passions, as you begin to pursue your dreams!

-THIRD; DO THE LIFE LESSONS IN THE ORDER THEY ARE IN THE WORKBOOK, NOT THE ORDER THEY ARE IN MY BOOK. I've prioritized the life lessons in the workbook.

For instance, by doing lesson #11 second, you work on "finding your purpose"..... Which is the most fundamental starting place for all of us. Likewise, Lesson #1 - "tweaking your dream" will come later in the workbook. There's no sense talking about tweaking a dream/goal, until you isolate and strive towards one to begin with!

Read and enjoy the book. Then take this journey with me! Let's really examine the 28 life lessons and learn how to apply them to your life, in order to attain your greatest potential!

Let's get started!

TABLE OF CONTENTS

TAKE THIS SURVEY:

http://www.dannypettry.com/30dayworkbook.pdf

APPLYING THE LIFE LESSONS TO YOUR LIFE

BECOMING YOUR OWN DRIVING FORCE!

"Ability is what you're capable of doing. Motivation determines what you do. Attitude determines how well you do it." -Lou Holtz (Coach/Sportscaster)

Workbook Introduction

My book, "Among the Giants" (and this companion journal), are not about carrying on a family legacy, fulfilling your parent's ambitions, or pursuing a goal just because it's always been expected of you. Instead, I have intended to create life lesson tools for you.... Tools that will help you become the type of person who can determine and develop a plan of attack in pursuit of their own dreams & passions.

However, before you can even begin to use these materials effectively, you need to determine what your passion is in life. Right now, today, what gets you excited just thinking about it? What "lights up your eyes" when you talk to others? Dreams & passions may change or take another direction in the future, but it is important to have a special goal to shoot for right now!

If you are a young person, this can be an overwhelming concept (What you're having for lunch may be your biggest focus and/or decision of the day!). I get it. But I also get that it is important to make decisions and have goals that are in the near future, instead of a million years away on some "adult" timeline in the back of your head.
An important part of the learning curve for you, is

figuring out how to "purpose" yourself towards something exciting and great! Only then can you begin to learn how to adapt, modify, and tweak what you've been working hard towards, as life's changes happen. I will show you how I've done that in my life, and I will give you examples on how to do that in your own. As you apply the life principals and strategies in my book to your own pursuits, you also learn how to critically evaluate what you're doing and determine whether it is working for you or wasting your time!

Slowly, the life strategies you are practicing and adopting, become a part of who you are, and they impact how you approach your own life as well as how you see the world. See if this isn't true.

*<u>ANSWER THESE QUESTIONS</u>, THEN COME BACK 3, 6, & 9 MONTHS AFTER PRACTICING THE LIFE LESSONS, AND ANSWER THEM AGAIN: (See Appendix A)

-Do you see a problem as a set back, or is it an opportunity? Why? How? Explain.

-Do situations control how you react, or do you choose your own responses to any situation? Give 2 examples:

-Do you respect others? How does that "look"? Explain?

-Do you respectfully stand up for yourself and teach others how to treat you? What does that "look" like?

-Do you notice and engage with the people around you that others "don't see"? (The custodian at school, the kid who has a hard time fitting in, the cashier at the market, the neighbor that suffers from Alzheimer's etc.) Give 2 examples:

1)

2)

-Does your economic/social/racial (etc.) background act as a stumbling block or excuse for you to NOT move forward, or do you take complete responsibility for your life and the future you can carve for yourself---- despite those issues?

These are just some of the questions you will be asked to reflect on as you take a hard look at yourself, and evaluate what you need to be doing in order to have the most exciting life possible! I'm honored to be on this journey with you, and I know you will discover just how unique and amazing your life can be!

Life Lesson #5
"Attitude is Everything!"

"Everything can be taken from a man but one thing: the last of human freedoms - to choose one's attitude in any given set of circumstances, to choose one's own way."

-Viktor E. Frankl

LESSON #5 REVIEW:

Attitude Is Everything! That is the most important life lesson in this book. You have to take 100% responsibility for your own life. If you don't wrap your head around this one, none of the other life lessons really matter. If you only get one, this is the one to get!

The more I experience in my life, the more I am convinced that attitude <u>truly</u> is everything. Bad things happen to us, there's no way around it..... However, if you become the master of your own personal attitude, you will be the one in control of your perspective and feelings moving forward in life. You will undoubtedly have a happier and more successful future!

Having a good attitude and always looking for the good can be a tough habit/quality to develop within yourself............but I can promise you, it is so worth it! Remember, having a good attitude in a <u>bad situation</u> is a choice, and the ball is in your court.

Choose wisely.

AUTHOR COMMENT:

My dad always told me that 'attitude is everything' when I was growing up. During the summer, we'd often watch a lot of Little League baseball games together, and I learned early on that dad had a different way of looking at the game. He didn't focus on the plays themselves (good or bad), rather he would watch how the players responded to the plays they were involved in.

Let me explain. He wasn't focused into who got the big hit, made the clutch catch, or dove into home plate for the game win. Instead, he looked to see what their attitude was when the sports "disasters" hit. When they struck out, missed a ground ball or got picked off. Did they hustle off the field? Did they chase down the ground ball? Did they hit their teammates hand and hustle to the next position? Or... did they argue with the umpire? Yell and blame their teammates? Slam their bat? Ignore their teammate as they stormed by?

Dad taught me that a players attitude, when times got tough, would determine their level of success in sports, and more importantly, in their life.

Often, we are unable to control what happens to us. However, we can control how we respond in every situation. Sports provide a beautiful illustration on how we should behave in our everyday lives. When unforeseen things befall us, sometimes we don't always know how to handle them. Your challenges may be different than mine, but we've all faced them. It's easy to want to blame someone (or something) beside ourselves, but that won't change anything. The key is to take 100% responsibility for your own life, and choose to look for the positive in every situation. Don't get bitter, get better! Turn that negative into the best thing that ever happened to you.

It's all a matter of your attitude, and the beautiful thing about that is, nobody can choose what your attitude will be except you. Not your parents, teachers, friends, siblings, or anyone else. ONLY you. How we respond in ANY situation, is the ONE thing we can control. I can promise you this much, if you learn to become the master of your own attitude, you will live a happier and much more successful life! It's not going to be easy; you aren't always going to want to find the positive when the going gets tough. Learning to challenge yourself to look for opportunities to shine, in the hard times, will make an enormous difference in your life.

Attitude is everything!

YOUR REFLECTIONS ON LIFE LESSON #5:

Give an example of when you totally reacted to something negatively when it happened:

Did you react this way out of anger, hurt, or frustration?

How did the situation end up? Did it improve

anything by reacting poorly? Did it make you feel good or bad 30 minutes after the incident? Why do you think that is?

If you could go back and redo your reaction, how would you handle it?

What do you think the outcome would have been? Better or worse?

It is often said that, "Hindsight is 20/20". What do you think that means?

Give an example of when you totally reacted to something in a positive way, with a good attitude:

What motivated you not to "flare up" or react poorly?

How did the situation end up? Did it improve anything by reacting well? Did it make you feel good or bad 30 minutes after the incident? Why do you think that is?

As you evaluate the situation, are you glad you

handled the incident that way? Why or why not?

How would, having reacted "poorly" in this situation, made the outcome look different?

Wouldn't it be nice if you knew beforehand what your reactions would do in a situation, 30 minutes after it's over?
As you evaluate the impact of your reactions during these times, you will most definitely learn the various ways a situation can look different, by which reaction you chose......

PERSONAL APPLICATION:

"A healthy attitude is contagious but don't wait to catch it from others. Be a carrier." -Tom Stoppard (actor)

Pick one situation where you habitually respond poorly (that you now want to improve/show some maturity in).
What is it?

What is your usual response (which isn't working or improving the situation)?

How does this response worsen the problem?

What are 3 things you can do which are better/more mature responses, which may cause a better outcome?

How would it feel to you, seeing things change due to a different attitude from you?

Would this feel empowering to you? Why?

How important do you think your choice of attitude is in empowering you, and keeping you in charge of your life?

CHOOSE EVERYDAY, WITH EVERY DECISION, TO BE THE MASTER OF YOUR OWN ATTITUDE! THERE IS NO OTHER POSITION YOU CAN TAKE WHICH GIVES YOU THE POWER TO ACT, REACT, AND MOVE FORWARD, AS WHEN YOU COURAGEOUSLY MAKE THE CHOICE TO HAVE A GOOD ATTITUDE!

Life Lesson #11
"Finding Your Purpose"

"If you can't figure out your purpose, figure out your passion. For your passion will lead you right into your purpose." –Bishop T.D. Jakes

LESSON #11 REVIEW:

Many of us go through our entire lives, and never find our true purpose. Sadly, a life with no purpose can feel like a wasted and lonely existence. Like a successful company, our lives should have a mission statement which summarizes the most important, singular goal we desire to achieve.

This can be hard to nail down, especially when you are young and still figuring out what you love to do.
If you could roll the thing you wanted your life to be into one or two sentences, what would it be?
A few questions you can might yourself are: "When do I feel the happiest?" "What brings me the most joy?" "When do I feel the most alive?"
Once you are able to answer these questions, a personal life mission will begin to emerge. Don't feel bad if you're unsure of your mission just yet. It can take awhile to figure out, and it can change a bit over time. However, now is the time to start thinking

along those lines. Get a head start while you are young!

AUTHOR COMMENT:

When I finally was able to verbalize my own personal mission statement, it changed my life! It gave me purpose and it brought clarity into my life. Before then, I was a little bit lost. I was focused on basketball, but I didn't know how pursuing it further would bring me the fulfillment I craved.

When I had a "Lightbulb Moment" and saw how I could use my platform of acting and basketball to share my story, suddenly the activities I loved became game changers! The thought of writing a book for teens, and going on the road to share my underdog story, both excited and scared me! BUT...I knew I was put here to do those things, and no matter what, I was going to make it happen! Sacrifices and dry stretches were aplenty, but I knew NOTHING was going to stop me. I'll admit it; the thought of speaking in front of thousands of people was extremely intimidating, especially talking about your struggles and mess-ups! Yet no matter how difficult, the one cool thing about finding my purpose was - the way it made the rest of my decisions easier!

Each time I was faced with a new choice, I would come back to my personal mission statement and ask myself, "Does this fall in alignment with my purpose?" If it did then I would say yes, if it didn't, I moved on to the next thing. Realizing what I was put here to do, changed my life! It put me on a new and exciting path, a path I never expected to be on.

I'm not in the NBA like I originally planned, but I now use basketball and my own unique set of skills to travel the world and impact the lives of others....... and I'm doing it all on my own terms! I encourage you to create your own personal mission statement. Get a target to shoot for! I know it can change your life, just like it did mine.

Isolating Your Dream:

It is easier to follow your dreams when you are focused early and know what you want! That is more than half the battle. Yet finding that passion can be hard for some people.

I (once again) recommend an online assessment for everyone, but especially those of you who are having a hard time figuring out who you really are and what you really have a passion for. This is an online, self-discovery assessment which can give you some incredible insight into yourself, and what you think/feel which you might never have realized about yourself before. The Author, Danny Pettry (A recreational Therapist) has given permission for anyone to download and print the pages, and I highly recommend it.

http://www.dannypettry.com/30dayworkbook.pdf

YOUR REFLECTIONS ON LIFE LESSON #11

After taking this survey, what is the most interesting thing you learned about yourself?

Did anything about this self-survey surprise you? What?

Trouble you? What?

Excite you?! What?

How will any of these answers in the survey, affect the direction you want to move in to pursue your dreams?

Does this give you a clearer picture of how you want to move forward?

Is that different than you expected? How?

What are 3 of the most valuable things you learned about yourself from taking the survey, which will help you moving forward?

PERSONAL APPLICATION

The funny thing about dreams & passions are, how they can be any of these 3 things, or a combination:

1 - Extremely shallow and/or temporary
        -OR-
2 - Foundationally motivating from childhood
        -OR-
3 - That in-between place... you are pursuing a goal over the long haul, and somewhere along the way, your focus changes and you have a new or expanded direction where you want to focus your life and energy!

That 3rd one is called "adjustment", or "tweaking" a dream, and I will go into that later in the workbook.

The first dream is what I call "fun, kids stuff". It's perfectly okay and totally appropriate for kids. They want to be a fireman, a princess, a teacher, a cop, a doctor... fill in the blank. It is always changing as they grow, and is part of their natural development. Healthy. Normal. Pretend.

The second type of dreaming can actually happen when you are a child, or any age/stage of a person's development. It's what I call "the real deal". (For some, it is actually in <u>retirement</u> that they have their greatest satisfaction in pursuing their interests and passions. That's sad to me, but better late than never.) Examples of these types of dreams are:
-Dancing ballet all through childhood, going to dance camps in the summer, and wanting to be a ballerina professionally.

-Having "play" doctor equipment as a child, looking at & loving physical anatomy books, and always being the one to bandage up your playmates. This kid always wanted to be a Doctor.

-Having a house full of animals as a child and always loving the responsibility of their care. Later, getting a weekend job on a hobby ranch. Being a Vet would be a dream come true.

-Writing stories for your grandchildren over a period of years, and finally getting them published as you pursue writing full time.

The biggest difference between the 1st type of "kids" dream, and the 2nd type of "real deal" dream, is the way a person pursues that dream. Kids give up and go on to the "next thing", but real dreams have a life all their own.

As you work hard, learn more, get to the "next step" of growth in your passion, you develop a discipline/nurturing relationship with it, and your dream begins to seem a little more attainable.

You have done one step at a time of the work needed to succeed, and that makes the leap forward that much more possible, because of the "smaller" steps already taken.

You see yourself in training, getting better, smarter, and more accomplished.

WHAT IS YOUR DREAM/OR WHAT IS YOUR LIFE PURPOSE?

Complete the Following:
DATE:

Like I asked previously: Right now, today, what gets you excited just thinking about it? What "lights up your eyes" when you talk to others?

At this point in time, can you see yourself pursuing this dream your whole life?

What would make you stop?

What will make you keep going?

NOTES TO SELF ON LIFE LESSON #11:

Life Lesson #16
"Embracing Your Uniqueness"

"Being different is a revolving door in your life where secure people enter and insecure exit." – Shannon L. Alder (author)

LESSON #16 REVIEW:

Out of the 7 billion people in the world there's no one just like you. How crazy is that? You are one of a kind and it might just be the thing you don't like about yourself which can help make you stand out and be great. Oftentimes, it's human nature to hide our insecurities, and be ashamed of our differences. Yet, when we learn to embrace our uniqueness and become comfortable and confident in our own skin, that's when we really start to shine! Learn to identify and use your unique differences to your advantage....... because, nobody is quite like you.

AUTHOR COMMENT:

As a kid, sometimes I would get frustrated when others didn't agree with me or think the same way that I did. One time I shared these thoughts with my dad and he told me, "If everyone was like you and me, it would be a pretty boring world to live in". That insight has stuck with me. Variety is the spice of life, and learning to view others as 'characters' instead of 'idiots', can make life a whole lot more entertaining and funny.

Once I learned to laugh and get a kick out of others and their differences, I began relaxing more around them! A simple perspective shift made a huge difference for me. This helped not only on how I viewed other people, but also on how I saw myself.

Growing up wasn't easy as the 'shorty' in school and on the basketball court. I was different, and not necessarily in a good way, to the thinking of many.

However, I slowly began to embrace who I was, and I began to realize that my differences could give me an advantage in the game of basketball, of all places! By being low to the ground, I could dribble quicker, do ball-handling on defense which annoyed my opponents, and get under people - which gave me the edge on getting foul calls from the referees.

By embracing my uniqueness, I was able to do some pretty sweet things that other people couldn't do. So, as I began working within my "wheel house", I played to MY own strengths, and brought something different to the game. Crowds were entertained, and many who had made a quick/shallow review of my abilities, soon became my biggest supporters!

Suddenly my shortcomings (literally) didn't hinder what I brought to the court!

What 'disadvantages' do you have that could be turned into your biggest asset?

Learn to love the things that make you different, and look for how those differences can play to your advantage! Get ready to learn that, surprisingly, you are awesome and unique just the way you are!

YOUR REFLECTIONS ON LIFE LESSON #16

As you look at your dreams/passions/goals, what are the greatest shortcomings or obstacles you possess, which you think "sabotage" your efforts towards your goals?

Have any of these things been too difficult to overcome?
Why or why not?

Have you stopped trying because of these shortcomings?

If you have stopped, how do you feel about giving up due to those obstacles?

Have you ever pushed through a personally limiting attribute anyway?

Explain how that felt to you:

Did you eventually succeed?
If so, what did that teach you?

PERSONAL APPLICATION

Thinking outside the box, how can you view your "liability" in a different way? In other words, how can a personal shortcoming help you play to the abilities you DO have?
Give 3 - 5 ways to see this problem in a positive light:

What will have to change in order for you to incorporate these new ideas?

How does having these new options feel to you?

Does this encourage you to keep pushing through a perceived difficulty? How? Why?

In what way can you apply this attitude to other areas of your life that are problematic?

Life Lesson #10
"Taking Complete Ownership of Your Life"

"Responsibility is accepting that YOU are the cause & the solution of the matter." -Pinterest

LESSON # 10 REVIEW:

This is one of the most important life lessons in my book. Unless you master this one, none of the other's will make much of a difference.

You have to take 100% ownership for you life. Though it's easy and tempting to want to play the victim card, blaming everyone and everything else for your problems, it's time to change that thought process.

As you begin to realize, that nearly everything going on in your life right now is the result of a choice that you've made, you can become the master of your destiny. YOU are in control.

As you face overwhelming circumstances, sometimes you will be at a lost on just how to handle things. Ultimately though, you have two choices:
You can get bitter and be the victim, or you can get better and be the victor.

Hard situations will arise in your life, that is a guarantee....... but you have the power to either let that situation define and ruin you, or allow it to push you on to be better and greater! If there is something in your life you don't like, you are the one who will actually have to do something about it.

Once you begin to take 100% ownership for your life, you will start to see dramatic changes.

AUTHOR COMMENT:

A big key to success for me, was my personal unwillingness to accept what other people told me I could and couldn't do with my life. When I was told I couldn't be a basketball player, I decided that I was going to be the one who determined if I would be able to do that or not. Then, I went out and put in the work, and eventually proved them all wrong.

 This same choice has presented itself to me many different times, and in a variety of different ways. In each situation, I decided to dictate to myself (personally), what I could or couldn't do, and that has made an amazing difference!

PLEASE, don't buy into other's critique of you. You can smile and thank them for their opinion, then use their negativity for a little extra fuel in your fire!

Learning to take 100% responsibility for you life, puts you in the driver's seat, and allows YOU to determine the outcome of many situations. Though that can be challenging and scary, it's a great feeling to be in control of your own destiny! Don't let your life be simply accepting what other people think it should be.

Here's the thing: if you don't write it nobody will

ever read it, if you don't speak it nobody will ever hear it, if you don't create it nobody will ever see it, and if you don't change it...... it will always be the same. Your life will either be lame or legendary. So once again, the choice is up to you.

Choose wisely.
Attitude is everything!

YOUR REFLECTIONS ON LIFE LESSON #10

"There's no point in me blaming you for what's wrong in my life". -Joyce Meyer

Name an area where you have <u>not</u> taken ownership in your life:

What excuse/s do you use to not take ownership of that area?

Do you see yourself as a victim?

How does that make you feel?

Can you see the situation improving without you taking action?

NOW, Name an area where you <u>have</u> taken ownership in your life:

How did that happen?

What does that "look" like?

How does that make you feel about yourself?

PERSONAL APPLICATION

"I am not a product of my circumstances. I am a product of my decisions."
-Stephen Covey

Where is that one place in your life, where you need to take action on right now?

Name 3 ways you can get around the obstacles that face you.

If those don't help, name 3 more ways:

And continue to do that until you succeed. Failure is NOT an option! Take ownership of your life. Stop blaming others, the system, the weather, the lack of time, etc.

OTHER THOUGHTS AND OBSERVATIONS ON THIS LIFE LESSON:

Life Lesson #3
"START TAKING ACTION!"

"Even If you're on the right track, you'll get run over if you just sit there." —Will Rogers

LESSON #3 REVIEW:

A huge hurdle to overcome in the pursuit of your dream, is overcoming your hesitancy to move out of your "comfort" zone into the unknown. This Life Lesson speaks to the importance of not allowing your fears to paralyze you into inaction. You have to learn how to <u>keep pushing</u> yourself out of that familiar "nest". It feels safe and secure to stay in the same place, but if you want to achieve your dreams and live an extraordinary life, you HAVE to learn to take a leap of faith...... and build wings on the way down!

AUTHOR COMMENT:

Often, when I hold an event, I will do something I saw Jack Canfield do at a convention. I hold up a $100 bill and ask the audience "Who wants this?" What happens is always very interesting to me. Nearly everyone gets excited, yelling that they want the bill, and may even jump up and down! While all that is happening, I just stand there, holding up the $100 bill, and wait patiently. Eventually someone will muster up the courage to get out of his/her chair and run up and take it out of my hand. Boom! Just like that, I'm a $100 poorer.

I always wonder, why everyone doesn't come up and try to take the money from me? Or why it always takes so long before someone makes their move? What makes this person different from the others? Do they possess some special quality that none of the others have?

I've come to this conclusion: most people waste entirely too much time worrying about what other people think of them. A lot of kids (even adults) are paralyzed with the fear that other people are going to judge them. That fear alone keeps them from taking action to chase their dreams.

The person who usually comes to the stage and grabs the money from me, is typically the class clown, or a super out-going kid who isn't afraid to look stupid.

These folks aren't scared to fail!

They aren't afraid I am going to make a joke out of them, tell them to sit down, and get laughed at by the rest of the school. Their lack of fear to be deemed 'stupid' or 'different' makes them $100 richer and the envy of their friends.

What's the take away lesson? No one will EVER accomplish anything of value, or reach their dreams, without taking action! Letting others opinion dictate what you will or won't go for in your life, is what will keep you locked into the same old place...

Who cares what other people think? What other people think about you...... is none of your business! Let them think whatever they want..... and then just go out and be great! Even if you fail the first time, you will just be back where you started from... so your life won't be any worse. Why not just go for it? What do you have to lose?!

I've learned through the years, that if I "waited" for just the right time to make my move in the direction of my dreams, I'd still be standing in the same spot! Even though timing is an important element to consider and a strategic element to use, there is hardly ever the "perfect" time, amount of money available, or a non-conflicting personal schedule. I've discovered that often, if I didn't act, the opportunity before me passed. The biggest factor in winning vs. losing is recognizing an opportunity and "going for it". You can't let fear cripple you into inaction.

YOUR REFLECTIONS ON LIFE LESSON #3:

-What are 3 opportunities which came your way, that you didn't take advantage of?

-What were the reasons/excuses that the opportunity slipped by?

-How did you feel?

-What are 3 opportunities which came your way, that you DID take advantage of?

-How did you feel?

-What are your 3 biggest fears as you pursue your dream?

-Would any of these fears coming true, destroy your dream or the direction you want to go? How or Why?

-What areas of your life do you use as an <u>excuse</u> to not take action towards your dream?

-How long have you used these excuses?

-How do you see these excuses disappearing?

PERONAL APPLICATION:

"If you have a dream, don't just sit there. Gather courage to believe that you can succeed and leave no stone unturned to make it a reality."
-Roopleen (author)

1) Name 3 to 5 ways you can confront your fears, and begin to take action in your life:

2) Name 3 to 5 things you can do, right now, to take action towards the future you want:

3)   Name 3 to 5 things you can make strategic plans to do in the next few weeks. Analyze the steps you need to take to reach that goal. (See example in Life Lesson #12, Practical Goal Setting)

*ADDITIONAL NOTES TO YOURSELF:

Life Lesson #2
"Going ALL In"

"If you aren't going all the way, why go at all?" -Joe Namath/Football Great

LESSON #2 REVIEW:

By examining the lives of many successful people, an undeniable theme that tends to emerge is their willingness to continue to push forward regardless of the setbacks encountered. These people seem unstoppable! They are "all in" in the pursuit of their dream. They have also built their successes layer upon layer, as they took each step necessary for their dreams to be a reality. They learned to believe in themselves, not because of some false sense of pride, but because they have proven over time that they were both capable, and determined to find any possible way around obstacles! A total commitment, in the direction of your dream, is the most important 1st step you will take in living out that dream.

AUTHOR'S COMMENT:

This is the place to begin to see your dream in a broader context. I take encouragement from other people's lives, those who have given 100% effort, generally when the odds are stacked against them. There are a series of failing/succeeding cycles in every endeavor. Winners have simply learned that you "push" through the failures until the "wins" begin to increase.

There have been many times in my life where I have made the decision to go all in. Oftentimes it was scary, but I'm so glad I did!

The day I decided to become the best basketball player I could be..... I went all in. I had a basketball in my hand 24/7, I ate nutritiously, I had a good sleep routine, I studied The Greats, and I did everything I could, to become the best that I could be. I wasn't just going through the motions; I would not do anything less than my best everyday.

When I first decided to try my hand as an actor, I saved up the money, and moved down to Los Angeles. I didn't have a clue of what I was doing, or how I would make money (let alone survive in the big city), but I went for it! I was committed to figuring it out... and that's what I did. If you put your mind to it, you can figure out just about anything, you just have to want it bad enough.

I quickly learned that I needed to put together an original basketball (trick) routine in order to book commercials, movies, and TV shows......... I went all in. I put in the hours, (oftentimes late into the night in questionable and unsafe neighborhoods at night) and didn't stop until I mastered every trick I practiced. Again, I went all in. I made the decision to be what I felt was great, and I didn't stop until I had achieved what I set out to do.

Finally, when I realized my passion in life was to inspire others with my underdog story (through speaking, books and entertaining), I knew I would only be successful if I decided to go all in. I researched the industry, contacted the top people in my field, wrote a book, and did all the work necessary to put myself on the map as a great motivational speaker. I didn't want to be average; I wanted to be the best. Remember, no one can do your push ups for you. Going all in means working your butt off. But if you are moving with passion towards your dream, I think you'll find that it's not work at all, and it's so exciting to see your progress!

YOUR REFLECTIONS ON LIFE LESSON #2:

1) Think of 3 people whom you admire or wish to emulate:

1) What might these 3 have in common with each other?

1) What differences do they have?

4) Do a brief Google search on what they say their struggles were in order to be successful in their lives.
Regardless of the individual struggles, what common theme did they all mention when they dealt with those struggles?

PERONAL APPLICATION:

- What are the greatest "take aways" you can learn? What successful ways did these people approach the roadblocks and challenges in their lives?

- How can, or does, this relate to your life?

- What are 2 or 3 major obstacles you can see in your pursuit of your dream?

- What are some PRACTICAL steps you can take to help you overcome those obstacles?

- How does making the decision to be "ALL IN", help you to take a "step by step approach" in overcoming obstacles to your dream?

Make the decision to Be All In when you are Ready:

I Am, "ALL IN", in the Pursuit of My Dream!

THIS IS MY DREAM:

My Name:

Today's Date:

Life Lesson #8
"Getting Self Motivated"

"Wanting something is not enough. You must hunger for it. Your motivation must be absolutely compelling in order to overcome the Obstacles that will invariably come your way." -Les Brown (Businessman)

LESSON #8 REVIEW:

It's awesome to have a supportive team on your side whether it is your family, friends, coaches or teachers. Unfortunately, that can only get you so far. At a certain point, it's on you to motivate yourself. What is driving and fueling your desire to be great? If you don't know the answer, you better figure it out soon... otherwise you more than likely won't stick with it.

It's no fun getting up at 5AM to get extra workout time, in before school. If you aren't self-motivated, after a week you'll be hitting the snooze button. Personal desire makes all the difference to achieving your goals, and it helps find the 'why' behind what you are doing, and what it is you want to do.

For instance, why do you desire getting good grades? Is it to get into the college of your choice? Or, are you applying for a scholarship? Maybe you get paid money for every 'A' you get?
Whatever the reason, find the 'why' to help you stay focused. It can help you power through those days when you don't want to put in the work. We all have those times where we "aren't feeling it".
Remember this: do today what others won't, so tomorrow you can do what others can't!

AUTHOR COMMENT:

Self-motivation can be a tricky thing. If possible, it's better to work with other people when you are pursuing greatness i.e. a workout partner, a study buddy, etc. Having another like-minded person will motivate you, and hold you accountable for doing the things you don't always feel like doing (but know you need to).

When a friend is checking in on your progress each week, it will motivate you to handle your business.... you don't want to let that person down. But... to be truly great, the motivation has to eventually be coming from inside of you.

We live in a world where many parents push their kids to be the best at different things: a sport, an instrument, singing, scholastics, etc. There can be a lot of pressure to excel; sometimes in an area you don't even have an interest.

I encourage you to have an honest conversation with those in your life who have other goals for you. Help them to understand and support your dreams, and try to always do those things that bring you the most happiness! Your true motivation will come when you are doing what you love, and you find your 'why' behind it.

When you find what you love, it will be so much more exciting. You will find your motivation within that love, and it will push you to be great!

YOUR REFLECTIONS ON LIFE LESSON #8

Name 3 things in your life that you would like to improve on, excel in, or be the best at!

On a scale from 1 -10 (10 being the highest), how would you rate yourself on your motivation to succeed in those three areas?

What personal rewards to you get from each of those 3 things? (Personal satisfaction, admiration from others, a chance to "move up the ladder" in that area to something better, etc.?

Which of these 3 areas are you the most motivated in?
Why do you think that is?
Which area are you the least motivated in? Why do you think that is?

Which area would you like to see the most improvement in? Why?

PERSONAL APPLICATION

People often say that motivation doesn't last. Well, neither does bathing, that's why we recommend it daily." -Zig Ziglar

Pick 1 area you want to work on. What kind of rewards can you give yourself, as you are working hard to improve, that will help you stay at it?

Why is it so important to make sure that the one area you pick is something you really love?

Name 3 things you can do that will help motivate you to "stick with it":

Promise yourself right now, "If I run into any discouragement, any fear, any failure, I will not quit until I have completed my commitment".

Signature: Date:

Life Lesson #12
"Setting Goals"

"A goal should scare you a little & excite you A LOT!" - Joe Vitale

LESSON #12 REVIEW:

If you don't know where you are going, sadly, you'll probably get there. It's awesome to have dreams, and big dreams at that. But the key to achieving those big dreams is to have goals.

-Goals that you write down.

-Goals that can be measured.
  Break it into baby steps

-Goals that you put a time limit on.
  Find a buddy and say, 'annoy me until I accomplish this next baby step.'

*These are things anyone can do, but most people won't. However, if you choose to, they will honestly make an enormous difference in your life.

AUTHOR COMMENT:

I love setting personal goals for myself! I'm kind of a goal-making fanatic. It's fun to feel challenged and that's all a goal is, a challenge to see if you can do something!

They say, 'success leaves clues'. If there's one thing that the majority of successful people have in common it's this: they set goals. They set goals and set a time for when each goal must be completed. They write goals in first person. They read them the first thing when they wake up in the morning and before they go to bed at night. They hang them in a place where they can see them every day (I used to hang mine in my locker at school).

I used to write some really big goals! Goals that I actually thought were unrealistic, but which I felt I should still go for anyway. What was cool was - as I reached some of my smaller goals, the ones which seemed so distant and impossible suddenly didn't seem that far off! They seemed more realistic and attainable.

I still have big goals out in front of me, and aspirations that some might considered 'far fetched' and unattainable. However, I've learned over time, it doesn't matter what other people say or think. The only thing that matters is what I think.

I want to have my own show on TV. I want it to be called The LeBeau Show, and it will feature me and various friends crisscrossing the country, meeting teens and bringing them back to LA to hang and be mentored by celebrities and pro athletes. An easy thing to accomplish? Heck no. Yet I believe I can do it, and will not stop until it becomes a reality. It's a goal I am determined to accomplish, and by sharing this with you, I now have many folks (like yourself) who are going to hold me accountable.

If you (and others) frequently ask me, 'Hey Jesse what's going on with The LeBeau Show?' That will put motivating pressure on me to get it going! It's a tactic I think you should use as well. Tell friends

what goals you want to accomplish and the dreams you have. Make sure they bug you so that every day you do something to get closer to that goal.
That's what it will take to be great.
And you are great!

YOUR REFLECTIONS ON LIFE LESSON #12

Name that one thing you have identified (by working through the questions in this workbook) as being "THE DREAM" you would love to dedicate as much time and energy as possible to:

So, how does goal setting help you in making that dream happen?

Below is the process a young person would map out in order to realize their dream.
Read the following example of their attempt to pursue that dream, step by step, until it all becomes possible!

Put yourself into their place, as if it is your dream, and walk through the process with me in making a dream a reality!

PERSONAL APPLICATION

"Breaking Down a Dream" into the steps necessary to succeed:

Sample Dream: To Become a Famous Actor on Broadway.

So this is your dream! You are starting High School next year, and so these are some of your High School goals:

-Take drama every year

-Take Public Speaking in school

-Join the Debate Club

-Join the community Toast Masters chapter

-Be in 2-3 plays during each of your Freshman & Sophomore years

-Be one of the leads in 3 plays during both your Junior and Senior years

-Volunteer at your local community Theatrical Arts Center; be available to star in productions as well as learning everything you can "behind the scenes".

-Write & star in short plays for community talent nights

-Put clips on youtube (with parental permission of course)

-Read bios of your Heros in Theater (Learn their secrets to success)

-Contact those locally who can act as a mentor to you (drama coaches, active thespians who majored in theater in college, etc.)

ALSO, BEGIN TO DO THESE THINGS:

-Select several colleges that have strong acting programs. Download their requirements, and begin charting out how to meet those requirements while in your freshman year of high school.

-Apply for summer positions at drama camps

-Apply for a summer internship at a Broadway theater

These are just a few examples of what you can begin to do NOW to pursue your dream. Try to generate more to this list, just to get you thinking.

NOW:

How do you think that having specific goals (like those above) will help you going forward in pursuing your OWN dreams?

What insight have you gained when you think about applying this type of goal writing to YOUR OWN DREAM?

-BEGIN PLOTTING SOME GOAL SETTING LIKE THE EXAMPLE GIVEN, WHICH WILL HELP YOU OVER THE NEXT 4 YEARS TO GET TO YOUR GOAL/S.

-TALK ALL OF THIS OVER WITH PARENTS, TEACHERS, PEERS, COACHES, COUNSELORS, ETC.

-GET ALL THE IDEAS AND INPUT YOU CAN, AND MAKE OUT A STRATEGY FOR SUCCESS!

*ADDITIONAL NOTES TO YOURSELF:

Life Lesson #19
"Creating Good Habits"

"We become what we repeatedly do." -Sean Covey (Author: The 7 Habits of Highly Effective Teens)

"Character is, for the most part, simply habit become fixed." -C. H. Parkhurst

LESSON #19 REVIEW:

A major key for success in your life is creating positive habits. Whether you realize it or not, most of your day you are in 'auto-pilot' mode. From the things you eat, how much water you drink, how much sleep you get, how you think about relationships, and even if you brush your teeth or make your bed, etc. It's the series of little things we do throughout the day that define us, and either maximizes or limits our success. Learning the, "how to be consistent and disciplined" is huge.

The sooner you learn to create good positive habits the better the quality of your life will be. So be encouraged! No matter how old you are, it's never too early or too late to create rituals that will help you build your desired life. We become our habits, so choose wisely!

*Remember, with every decision you make... you are ultimately deciding the person you are going to be!

AUTHOR COMMENT:

I am obsessed with studying successful people, how they live their lives, and particularly the habits they have. I want to learn what they do differently which separates them from the rest of the pack. What makes them great, and most importantly, can I apply that to my life and get similar results?

If you want to be great at anything, find the people who are the very best, and see what it is they do. Watch your favorite athlete on Youtube, study interviews with your heros, read books from the leaders on your topic, join a study group with the kids who excel in the class you want to do better in, the list goes on and on...

Around fourth grade I realized there were things I could do that would give me an edge on the competition as a basketball player. I cut sugar out of my diet, I made myself throw the ball up 100 times (both left and right handed), and I'd do 100 calf raises before I would let myself go to bed. I had a set time for bed because I knew sleep was critical to recovery and success in school and sports. These are just a few examples.

One area I believe is critical to your success, or lack thereof, is how you choose to use your phone. As an actor, speaker, and someone who has a 'brand', social media and staying in contact with others is extremely important to my career. With that being said, I have certain parameters for my phone usage. I have a set amount of time that I allow myself to go on social media, I turn on airplane mode at night, etc.

Your phone can be a wonderful thing, or it can be something that wastes your time, keeping you from achieving your dreams. You can spend all day texting, tweeting, scrolling through feeds, and 95% of it is a time killer. The habits you develop with your phone will make or break you.

YOUR REFLECTIONS ON LIFE LESSON #19:

-Are your habits making you the person you want to be or keeping you in a place you don't want to be?

-Give a few examples of each

-What are 3 habits you KNOW you should lose?

-What are 5 habits you would love to incorporate into your life if you could?

-What priority would each of those habits have? Rate them 1-5.

-Who has the control to establish these habits? Why is that important to know going into establishing anything new, and potentially difficult?

PERONAL APPLICATION:

1) Write down all the habits you can think of which have put you in your current situation... both good & bad (Believe it or not, the habits you have now are responsible for putting you at your present state).

2) Pick an area of your life you want to improve in and write out what it looks like right now. Be detailed and honest!

-What habits could you develop which would help you attain mastery in those areas?

-What habits could you develop, which would increase your chances of being successful in School?

-What habits could you develop, which increase your chances of having better relationships in your home?

-What habits could you develop, which would help you gain and establish a circle of quality friends who all support and enrich each other's lives?

(I go into some of this at length in Life Lessons #13, 14, 18, 20, 23, & 24)

3) Write down what you want! What's the vision that gets you excited? "I want to save X amount of money". "I want to be in the best shape of my life". "I want to............ (Fill in the blank)

4) What new habits can you learn that will help you progress to your vision in part 3?

5) When will you spend extra time training/rehearsing/practicing?

6) What will your training consist of? What about your diet? Who will you train with? Be specific.

I encourage you to start with just one area of your life to begin building good habits. Once you get going in even one area you can build momentum that will carry over to other areas of your life!

Remember, a habit is something you do consistently until it becomes automatic. Without a doubt there will be times when you are tired, overwhelmed and just flat out not motivated. Don't become discouraged. We all face that.

Just remember, it takes approximately 6 weeks to establish a new habit. Everything gets much easier the longer you stick with it. The daily struggle to "force" yourself to hang in there, gives way to "now it's just automatic".

Life Lesson #7
"There's No Substitute for Hard Work"

"Success is dependent upon the glands - sweat glands." ~ Zig Ziglar

LESSON #7 REVIEW:

No one can do your push-ups for you, and that's a fact! Most of us want the quick fix......... take a pill to lose weight, get a surgery to change a part of the body, become famous for doing nothing overnight, and enjoy the perks (of any) success, without putting in the work.

WELL......It doesn't work like that (thank goodness), and I think that's a good thing. How much would you really appreciate your own successes if you didn't have to work hard for them? Certainly not as much as a goal you had to sacrifice time and effort for as you strove to become great and achieve your dream!

Your work ethic will either be your biggest asset, or your greatest downfall in life. We all have different skills and opportunities. What separates being good from being great, are those who are willing to roll up their sleeves, get down and dirty, and put in the work!

To become a master at anything, it has been said that you need 10,000 hours doing that thing. Talk about commitment! Like the wise Thomas Edison said, "Opportunity is missed by a lot of people because it is dressed in overalls and looks a lot like work".

The truth of the matter is this: if you want to be great at something, your work ethic is going to be the biggest factor to achieving it.

AUTHOR COMMENT:

I was never the most talented at anything growing up. Whether it was being the smartest in school, the best athlete, or just running around the outdoors fishing and hunting. I never had more natural ability than anyone else, but I did possess an insane work ethic and desire to be the best, which led me to put in more hours (practicing, studying, etc) than others. By doing that, I was able to excel in both sports and school. Hard work has been the key to success for me in my life.

It's easy to 'talk the talk', but is a whole other matter to 'walk the walk'. Anybody can talk a big game (and most people do), but it's the "doers" who take action, and actually make their own success happen. There will always be an excuse... You are sore, tired, injured, don't have enough money, live in the wrong neighborhood or city, don't have support from your friends or family, or... it's the wrong time of year...etc. There will never be the perfect time to do anything in your life. Successful people take action anyway! What are you willing to do to be successful? Go to bed and get up earlier? Exercise more? Eat better? What are you willing to give up to be successful? Friends who aren't motivated? Watching TV? Your cellphone? Social media?

We all have the same amount of hours in the day, but how you choose to spend those hours, either working hard or wasting time, are completely up to you. How bad do you really want your dreams to become your reality? Choose wisely, your choices decide who you will become.

YOUR REFLECTIONS ON LIFE LESSON #7

"The fight is won or lost far away from witnesses - behind the lines, in the gym, and out there on the road, long before I dance under those lights."
-Muhammad Ali (Boxing Great)

What are two things you were excited about once, but gave up on when the work effort was too much?

Were you relieved, frustrated, sad, etc. when you walked away from a previous pursuit? Explain why you felt that way.

Have you every wanted to go back and redo that decision? Did you? How did/does it feel with either decision?

Did you replace that goal/desire with another pursuit that you enjoyed more, found easier, had more satisfaction from? Explain.

What are two things, that really mattered to you, which you really worked hard at to master?

How successful were you?   How did that feel?

Are you still trying to improve and get better?

Are you pushing forward to a more advanced place in these dreams/goals? How or how not?

Are you still excited and motivated?

PERSONAL APPLICATION

"If you don't have time to do it right, when will you have the time to do it over?"   -John Wooden (Hall of Famer as a player and a coach)

What are 3 things you can do to improve your work ethic just generally in your life?

What are 3 things you can begin doing today which will help you consistently work smarter, in order to reach your goals?

What are 3 new things you can learn, and/or habits you can form, which will help you develop a better work ethic?

What values do you have that help you maintain a good strong work ethic? Are you honest? Do you have a positive attitude? Are you both reliable and responsible? Do you take initiative? Do you care about classmates/teammates and their opinions? Do you learn new skills, and are you a good "team" or group player when you need to be?

Name a couple ways you can incorporate some of these values and ideas into your life... to motivate you to work harder, and smarter!

How do any or all of these things help you train yourself into a "better work ethic"?

Are you excited about this process? Do you have confidence in yourself that you will follow through? What would help you to get to a place of personal enthusiasm to work hard for what you want in life?

If you aren't a self-motivated person by nature, name three things that you can do this week that will help you stretch and grow in this new area of strong work ethic:

Life Lesson #4
"Be Committed, Do the Work!"

"Hard work spotlights the character of people: some turn up their sleeves, some turn up their noses, and some don't turn up at all." – Sam Ewing

LESSON #4 REVIEW:

This lesson emphasizes how commitment and work are the greatest partnership in gaining success. Your commitment to your dream/goal, is directly linked to the work ethic you implement to pursue that goal! When you stick to a regiment, plan, or course of action until you've completed your task, you build a foundation for personal success.

All the blood, sweat and tears that go into that foundation continue to give you the platform necessary to keep building, block by block, until you reach both your short term and long term goals! Likewise, "quitting" is often the indicator of a person's lack of commitment to their goal. Either route; complete commitment to the work ethic needed to succeed, or choosing to quit along the way, you are 100% in charge of the decision.

AUTHOR COMMENT:

It's so true; we all fantasize about doing, creating, or accomplishing something incredible! Yet when it comes down to the work and time we need to put into our dream, we can waver. We often start out with a "New Years Resolution" attitude, but as roadblocks begin to pop up, the WILL to continue can greatly decrease. We have to remind ourselves that no one can do our pushups for us, and train ourselves to see obstacles as OPPURTUNITIES, learning to be creative when confronted with them. Perseverance is key.

I have committed to many different things over the years, and sometimes my friends made fun of me because they were a little strange for a kid! When I decided to cut refined sugar from my diet, I did it "cold turkey". Just stopped. Except for my one indulgence: Friday at Coldstone! Every Friday, I go and treat myself there! But... All week, there isn't any question about eating cookie's or taking the candy bar someone offers me, because I've committed to only eating sugar on Fridays, no exceptions.

The added benefit is: all week I look forward to Coldstone... and when I get that sucker, you better believe I enjoy every bite of it! It's the highlight of my week! Haha
By doing this, I stay healthier and appreciating the small things in life. Also, the discipline it creates helps me in so many other areas of my life. Committing creates discipline, and discipline can separate the good from the great. Learning self-control can also keep you from getting sidetracked by other "time wasting" activities.

If you really want to become the master of something, you need to develop a type of 'tunnel vision' and stay focused & committed to the prize!

YOUR REFLECTIONS ON LIFE LESSON #4:

- What were the 2 most recent goals you were successful with?

- What steps did you take to make that success happen?

- What setbacks did you experience along the way?

- What idea's, strategy's, or techniques helped you overcome the obstacles?

- Did you come up with any creative strategies that worked? What?

- Was there any trial and error involved in helping you develop a strategy that worked?

- On a scale from 1 to 10, how important do you think a failed, or many failed attempts, can help you refine a strategy that works? _____
Why did you give your own perseverance that score?

"I have not failed. I've just found 10,000 ways that won't work."
-Thomas A. Edison

-How can having the above perspective (quote) help you to push through the tough times?

PERSONAL APPLICATION:

"Maturity comes when you stop making excuses and start making changes". -Anonymous

-What are 2 obstacles you are now facing in pursuing your goal/s?

-What have you already tried in order to overcome these obstacles?

-Why do you think your attempts were unsuccessful? Did you break down your goals into "manageable" chunks? Did you attempt to bypass the necessary steps, and just push towards the finish line?

-Take a new look at your 2 unfinished goals. In what way can you approach them differently for a successful outcome?

-What are some new approaches in breaking these goals down into "manageable" chunks?

-Rewrite those 2 goals, and enumerate the steps you'll take to accomplish them. Give yourself a date to complete them so you have accountability built in. (Be realistic.)

1st Goal:

Steps I Plan to use to succeed:

Date 1st goal will be accomplished: _____

2nd Goal:

Steps I Plan to use to succeed:

Date 2nd goal will be accomplished: _____

How does doing this exercise change your perspective on goal setting?

Life Lesson #6
"Visualize It"

"I dream my painting and I paint my dream." – Vincent Van Gogh
(Artist)

LESSON #6 REVIEW

Wouldn't be great if we could know what was going to happen to us before it actually happened? Well, in some respects, we can. Our thoughts (negative and positive) have a big impact on our successes and failures.

Do you believe you are going to do well on that upcoming test? Do you think you will hit the game winning shot or do you expect yourself to make some crucial mistake that will cost your team the game? What you think AND what you see in your minds eye will make or break you!

Your mind is a powerful thing and has a profound effect on the outcomes you experience in your life. Self-fulfulling prophecy is very real and broken down in more simple terms means this: what you predict to happen usually happens.

Start practicing positive self-talk. Start expecting good things to happen in your life. Become an inverse paranoid. What you put out into the universe comes back to you, it is known as the law of attraction.

AUTHOR COMMENT:

Visualization has been a major key to success in my life. The first time I started visualizing the outcomes I wanted in my life, was when I heard it would give me the edge in sports. I read that many of the world's top athletes would envision the results they wanted in their upcoming games, so I decided to try it.

The results were dramatic! I would lie down before games, and see myself making the big shot, threading the perfect pass, or getting the game-winning hit in high pressure situations. Whatever I wanted to happen, I would make sure I saw those results. I learned to be as specific as possible. What color was the opposing team wearing? Who would I be facing specifically? How loud would the fans cheer? What emotions would I feel? The more specific I was, the better the outcome was.

Research shows that your mind can't tell the difference between what's really happening at any given moment, and what you imagine is happening, especially when you get your emotions involved. By going through this visualization process, I discovered I was actually more calm and confident during games. This was due partly to the fact that it felt like I had been there before, and I knew I would succeed.

You can do this in any area of your life. Got a big test coming up you are nervous about? Visualize yourself acing it and confidently answering the questions. Have a big presentation around the corner that is giving you anxiety? Take some time and see yourself presenting your information eloquently and impressing your classmates and teacher. You get the idea. See yourself succeeding. You are what you think!

"One man thought he could, the other man thought he couldn't.......................... They both were right!"

YOUR REFLECTIONS ON LIFE LESSON #6:

"You can't depend on your eyes when your imagination is out of focus."
~Mark Twain (Author)

Close your eyes and see in your mind all the awesome things you want in your life already happening!

What are some of those awesome things?

Why do you think you value them?

How can any of these things help you achieve your dreams?

What will it feel like to achieve any of those goals?

Who will be there to congratulate you?

Take some time visualizing your dream life; you have to see it to achieve it!

PERSONAL APPLICATION:

Pick one goal you want to reach. What is it?

How many steps will it take to reach that goal? List them?

Go through your list one by one, and while closing your eyes, see each of those things happening the way you want in your imagination.

Continue to practice this visualizing technique every day. Start seeing the details of how the actual experience will look and feel to you.

Add practice to visualization. See yourself walking through the steps necessary to succeed in this area.

Read more on visualization. There are many techniques that work for different areas. See what fits best for you!

Life Lesson #9
"Standing Up for Yourself"

"Once you embrace your value, talents and strengths, it neutralizes the negative, when others think less of you." -Rob Liano (Author/Speaker)

LESSON #9 REVIEW:

Standing up for yourself is crucial. Times will come in life, when others may try to take advantage of either your kindness or generosity. It's important to learn to take care of yourself first, before you spend energy looking out for the needs of others. You can't feel bad about it either.

Sometimes it's necessary to be selfish. Putting yourself first when it comes to your health is one of those times. Taking the necessary steps to recharge your batteries, getting enough sleep, and allowing yourself to still have the energy for working on the things you need to, are fundamental if you desire to live a healthy life.

Don't be afraid or apologize for putting yourself first in these critical areas of your life. By taking time to be the greatest version of yourself, you will then be able, in turn, to help others achieve greatness in their own lives!

As the wise saying goes: "I don't know the key to success, but I know the key to failure is to try to please everyone."

AUTHOR COMMENT:

I've had times in my life when others have tried to walk all over me and take advantage of me, for a plethora of reasons. Sometimes it was an employer; other times it was a (so called) 'friend', teacher, or coach. It came in many different forms. Often, others felt they had the upper hand - so they could get away with it - but I would not let that happen.

We all deserve respect, and we must insist on it from others in our lives. Remember, you can only be treated **how you allow** people to treat you. I've personally walked away from large paychecks, scholarships, teams, and even roommates. It wasn't even a close call.

Out of respect for myself, I've developed a standard by which I expect to be treated by anyone who is in my life. Likewise, I treat others the way I wish to be treated. It hasn't always been easy, but there is no dollar amount worth trading for your own self-respect. When you know you have been true to yourself, and also treated others fairly and kindly, you are able to walk forward in life in a balanced and strong way.

Don't be afraid to stand up for yourself, you might just find that others will respect you a lot more when you do.

YOUR REFLECTIONS ON LIFE LESSON #9

Name 3 situations where you have let others have control, where you haven't stood up for yourself or for what you want.

How has that made you feel? Angry? Sad? Disrespected? Relieved? Invisible? etc.?
Is that the type of relationship you would always want to have?

Many times we don't stand up for ourselves because we don't have the self-confidence that comes from within. Self-confidence can grow when we challenge ourselves and truly accomplish something we hadn't before!

Also, remember that a good attitude is infectious! If you are a positive upbeat person, others will be drawn to you and feel good around you. Your confidence will grow, and that in turn will help you "stand up for yourself" when it is necessary!

PERSONAL APPLICATION

"One of the greatest regrets in life is being what others would want you to be, rather than being yourself." -Shannon L. Alder (Writer)

Continue to work on those areas (you've identified in the workbook), which bring you satisfaction, maturity, self worth, and purpose! You will be better able to see yourself as talented and valuable, and stand up for yourself in the situations that need it!

NOTES TO SELF ON THIS LIFE LESSON:

Life Lesson #14
"Changing Your Sphere of Influence"

"If you hang out with chickens, you're going to cluck and if you hang out with eagles, you're going to fly." -Dr. Steve Maraboli

LESSON #14 REVIEW:

It has been said, "We can't pick our family, but we can pick our friends. Making friendships and having those closest to us be people of character, enthusiasm, and integrity, should be a lifelong goal!

We also need to surround ourselves with people we can be learning from. What individuals do you know who are where you would like to be in your life 5, 10, 20 years down the road? By associating with, and spending time with these individuals, you begin to pick up their thinking, their habits, their way of focusing, and their ability to move forward towards a goal or dream!

AUTHOR COMMENT:

I believe that a major key for me accomplishing my goals and getting closer to my dream, is surrounding myself with the right people. It's tempting to want to surround oneself with people who aren't as smart, good looking, or talented, because it makes us feel superior, playing into our ego. However, that isn't where the growth happens!

The smartest thing you can do is find people who are more accomplished than you! Surround yourself with people who will push you, encourage you, and inspire you! Find the friend that is so smart you have to look up words after you hang out with them, to figure out what the heck they were talking about! Be a sponge, you can learn from anyone if you are willing to approach it the right way.

Maybe you can learn what NOT to do, or what mistakes to look out for. If you want to take the shortcut to success here it is: find people who are already successful at what you want to do, and spend as much time around them learning as you possibly can.

You're welcome!

YOUR REFLECTIONS ON LIFE LESSON #14

-Combined with Life Lesson #13, next.

PERSONAL APPLICATION

-Combined with Life Lesson #13, next.

Life Lesson #13
"Surrounding Yourself with Great People"

"Whatever you do in life, surround yourself with smart people who'll argue with you."   -John Wooden

LESSON #13 REVIEW:

Show me your five closest friends and I'll tell you WHO you are. Arguably, we are the average of the 5 people we spend the most time with! This applies to how much money you make. who you are socially, what career you are currently in (or headed towards), and the condition of your relationships & family life.

The company you keep really says a lot about you, and plays a huge role in your success or failure in life. Do the people you associate with build you up and support you with positivity, or do they tear you down and discourage you from doing the things you believe in, hindering you from reaching your full potential?

AUTHOR COMMENT:

I've purposely surrounded myself with people who are more successful than me, and I've done it intentionally. When I was a scrawny, punk kid who thought he had some skills with a basketball, I played against the adults who kicked my butt and forced me to get better. I had to learn how to be stronger, faster and protect the ball (from bigger defenders). It made me sharper. When I wanted to do my best in school, I sat and hung out with the smart kids. I learned how they studied, and listened to the questions they asked. As a result, I got better grades.

Today, I surround myself with successful actors and people in entertainment, millionaires and billionaires, and the top speakers in the world!

Always recognize, early in your life, that there are many people who are better at the things you want to be great at, and learn – learn – learn from them!

It keeps you humble. It keeps you learning. It keeps you growing in your dreams.

Sometimes it's tempting to spend time around those who aren't as talented as you are. It makes you feel good to be the best in your little group, but that thinking is limiting and won't benefit you in the end. Find people who are great and supportive of you, and choose to have those people be the ones you spend your time with.

YOUR REFLECTIONS ON LIFE LESSON #13 & #14

-Name 3-5 people already in your life that are positive influences:

-Do these friends encourage you to do your best at things?

-Do they push you to try something new, and stick with it?   Give some examples:

-Are they happy at your successes, or is there jealousy?   How can you tell?

-Which of your teachers, coaches, neighbors, etc. show an interest in you and encourage you in your life?

-What clubs or organizations at school (or in your community) do you have an interest in joining?
-Are these filled with people that would be a positive addition to your life?   How? Why?

PERSONAL APPLICATION (for #13 & #14)

-Make a list of all the positive people and activities already in your life:

-How can you spend more time involved with these people and activities?

-Make a list of future people and groups you'd like to connect with, which would add "positive energy" to your life.

Life Lesson #26
"Being Motivated by Your Haters"

"It is not the critic who counts; not the man who points out how the strong man stumbles, or where the doer of deeds could have done them better. The credit belongs to the man who is actually in the arena, whose face is marred by dust and sweat and blood; who strives valiantly; who errs, who comes up short again and again, because there is no effort without error and shortcoming; but who does actually strive to do the deeds; who knows great enthusiasms, the great devotions; who spends himself in a worthy cause; who at the best knows in the end the triumph of high achievement, and who at the worst, if he fails, at least fails while daring greatly, so that his place shall never be with those cold and timid souls who neither know victory nor defeat."

-President Theodore Roosevelt

#26 REVIEW:

No matter what you do in your life, often there is someone who is going to want to tear you down. That's just a fact. Also, the more you do and the more successes you have, the greater potential for negativity to escalate.

Let me be honest with you - that's the way it goes. You might be doing the must noble and unselfish thing in the world, and still, some people will find a way to speak negatively about it. You may be trying to cure cancer or traveling the world saving starving children, and still, some will flood your feed and inbox... saying what a horrible person you are. Brush it off. Don't let this stop you from living your purpose, and being great. Instead, let negative words motivate you, and push you to be even better and greater! Add it to your fire as fuel!

Proving others wrong can be a lot of fun, and may give you that little extra push you need at times. Harness that energy and use it to your advantage. It's always up to you to turn around what's negative, and use it instead for your very own good!

AUTHOR COMMENT:

In my life, I've had so many people try to stomp on my dreams and trash my goals. I wouldn't know where to begin making a list! Nevertheless, I am thankful. I just happen to be a guy who is super motivated by people telling me I CAN'T do something. It still motivates me to this day.

Recently I have been working on some big ideas in the TV world, and to say I am being ambitious would be an understatement. There have been many who have been vocal about my poor chance at success. But you know what? It doesn't matter. I'm still up every morning focused and working hard on my next dream. I'm still going for it! Like I said before, it's all just fuel for the fire.

A huge thing I've learned over time is this: Make sure you do the things you do, because they are what YOU want, and what YOU believe in. Simply trying to prove others wrong is fuel for the fire, but isn't the right motivation. There should always be the 'why' behind your efforts. At the end of the day, anything you do needs to be for you.

Also, don't let anyone stop you from setting out to do what it is you have in your heart! When the haters start chirping, just work that much harder to prove them wrong. The look on their faces when they see you succeed, well... That will be PRICELESS!

YOUR REFLECTIONS ON LIFE LESSON #26

-How easily are you swayed by the opinions of others? On a scale from 1 - 10 (10 being the most), rate yourself:

-Name two incidents where others opinions stopped you from pursuing a direction you wanted to go:

1)

2)

-What was done/said by them, which stopped you?

-How did you feel?

-How did you respond/react to them at that moment?

-Why was/is the opinion of this person/s important to you?

-What would have happened to you if you had pursued your desire anyway?

-Is that a reaction, which you might not like, but you could live with?

-If you could go back and redo the encounter, how would you handle it differently?

In the two previous life lessons (#13 & #14), I talked about surrounding yourself with "like-minded" people. Those people, who you admire, can learn from, and who help you build a positive self-image as well as positive relationships. Working on establishing those bonds, would be the most helpful when dealing with negative people and negative situations.

A supportive group of people, who have your back, can defuse even the most hostile critics in your life!

PERSONAL APPLICATION

-Pick one of the previous incidents you wrote about (at the start of this lesson), and let's examine it here:

-Did you have any idea that you might be treated the way you were? How or why?

-Did it catch you "off guard"?

-Give 3 responses you might have given to the person which would have helped the situation. (Ignored them, prepared a witty remark, used humor, etc.)
*Be specific on what words you would have used:

1)

2)

3)

-How might each of those responses have changed the outcome of the situation?

In the end, regardless of whether or not a different strategy stops a hater, don't allow someone else's opinion dictate what you do or don't do in your life.

As you get older, often these "Shut Downs" by others aren't even a personal put down. Something like this happened to me at a basketball audition (for a TV commercial) that I went to several years ago.

I had practiced my ball handling and "tricks" for a few days, and then headed to the local park where the auditions were being held outdoors. As I strolled up to the registration table, the producer looked me up and down, and informed me that they were actually, "looking for a black dunker for this particular commercial". Obviously he didn't want to waste his time with a short, little white guy. I was disappointed, but covered it completely with my response: I shook his hand, smiled, and said, "Well I'll be working on that"! We both laughed!

Learn to turn around a perceived "disrespect" with a sense of humor and a smile! Who knows, when this producer is looking for a small, white, ball handler.... I'll be his guy! I know I made myself memorable to him by just having a good attitude and a sense of humor!

NOTES TO YOURSELF ON THIS LESSON:

Life Lesson #17
"Learning when it's OK to be Selfish"

"Motivation is simple........ You eliminate those who are not motivated!" – Lou Holtz

LESSON #17 REVIEW:

Sometimes, it's okay to be selfish. In fact, it's good to be selfish at certain times. In order to best help others and make the greatest impact you can in this life, it's important to learn when this is okay.

Let me explain. You can't help others if you aren't healthy yourself. This means getting to bed at the right time - so you have the energy the following day for pursuing your dreams. This means eating good and exercising for health and energy. This means blocking out time to relax... having some 'you time', to recharge your batteries. These are just a few things to help keep you healthy physically, emotionally, and mentally. Sometimes you will also have to put other important things first; your career, your education, your relationships, etc.

At the end of the day, it's critical for you to determine the areas where you need to put yourself first. Once you grow into the best version of yourself (functioning at your highest level), you'll be able to accomplish more, and additionally, have the resources needed to help others be great as well. If you neglect yourself, putting others needs first all the time, you will never reach your full potential (and you'll inevitably develop burn out).

AUTHOR COMMENT:

It's can be exhausting always being the "nice guy". Often, while growing up, I felt pressure to continually do things for others first. I was a nice guy, and spent a lot of time listening to conversations I didn't want to hear, going to events I didn't want to see, and spending my time doing favors/catering to everyone else's needs.

I started learning how to be 'selfish' when it came to gym time. Friends would want to play full court, mess around playing 'bump' or 'horse', and then shooting crazy shots from half court. I knew this type of activity was a waste of time and wouldn't get me playing a better game... which was one of my goals!

Nope, half hearted play with the guys wasn't going to get me that college basketball scholarship. Friends would get really ticked off when I refused to mess around with them at the gym. Instead, I was choosing to be 'selfish' and serious with my time, and that was the best decision I could have made! It's helped me get to where I am today.

Don't be afraid to be selfish when it comes to making decisions about your own life, and the course you need to be on to fulfill your dreams. In the end, it's one of the most unselfish things you can do for your future.

YOUR REFLECTIONS ON LIFE LESSON #17

-Give two examples where you have let others keep you from using your time wisely:

-How did you make up for that lost time?   Were you able to?

-How inconvenient was that?

-How would you handle those two situations differently now? (Be specific in your answers.)

PERSONAL APPLICATION

-Name the ONE, main thing, you wish you could spend more time focusing on, and improving in:

-What are the 3 greatest roadblocks to accomplishing that?

1)

2)

3)

-Pick those three things apart 1 by 1! Give a thorough answer on how you can tackle each of those three roadblocks:

1)

2)

3)

*Now............. Begin to implement your ideas!

Life Lesson #18
"Developing Character"

"Character is the result of two things: Mental attitude and the way we spend our time." -Elbert Green Hubbard

LESSON #18 REVIEW:

Good character is a "choice" we are making every day of our lives. Whether you realize it or not, every time you make a decision (good or bad, small or large, right or wrong) you are setting a pattern and deciding who you are going to be in this life.

Good character is something we develop EVERY time we make a good decision, take the high road on issues, or put others before our own selfishness. Likewise, a lack of character happens when we make poor decisions. When we take advantage of others (often without them knowing), when we blame others for our own shortcomings, when we cheat - lie - steal etc., because the short term pay off makes us happy for the moment.

The reason we need to see how important every decision is, is this: it gets easier to make that same type of decision the second time, the third time, and so on. Before you know it, now you are "that guy". The one no one trusts or believes.

They say character is what you do when no one else is watching. I think that's a great litmus test. Are you the same person when no one else is around to see what you are doing? Learn what your absolutes are. Most of us (hopefully) have things we believe are wrong and would never do, such as: Leave a towel on the bathroom floor (ok maybe we would do that!), cheat on a math exam, throw a baby, drink and drive, etc., you get the idea. We can't always control what our <u>reputation</u> is with others, (because people lie and gossip), but we can control what our <u>character</u> is... and that will say everything about who we are.

Having strong, respectable character is the highest attribute a person can possess. Strive to be someone of high character and strong moral fiber. It will serve you well as you chase your dream, and it will show others that you are a person of integrity, strength, and trustworthiness. If you put the development of good Character first in your life, everything else will fall into place.

AUTHOR COMMENT:

I have a vivid memory of one particular time when I was around 8 years old. I was at the grocery store and the checker didn't ring up one of my items. I walked out thinking I had gotten a great deal! When I got back to the car, I told my older brother what had happened. He looked at me and said, "Your integrity isn't worth that $5 savings, go back in there and pay it right now".

It was a powerful lesson that really stuck with me. My brother was right. My reputation and character weren't worth a measly $5. In fact, there wasn't any dollar amount that could be put on replacing a lapse in character. Having the respect of others (because you choose to be a moral person) is a character quality that is priceless. No one can ever buy respect. Once you lose it, it's (often) gone forever.

YOUR REFLECTIONS ON LIFE LESSON #18

We talk about a person being of "Good Character" all the time. What do we mean by that? List the qualities that really describe good character:

Does a person have "good character" from birth?

How does one get it?

Share an incident that stands out in your mind when you made a decision that showed poor character choice:

What drove you to make that decision?

How did you feel afterwards?   Why?

Was it easier to make another "poor" decision after that, or was it harder?

PERSONAL APPLICATION

We all have areas that we need to improve upon in the area of character! Think of two areas that need the most attention in your own life. (i.e. true to your word, trustworthy, keeps someone's confidence & secretes, is known as a giver, is thoughtful to others, stands up for the less fortunate, doesn't put people down, not a bully but an encourager, does cheat, doesn't lie, doesn't steal, etc.)

What are your 2 areas?

Why do you think you struggle in those 2 areas?

What "reinforces" you continuing to behave in those 2 destructive ways?

In what positive ways do you see your life changing if you can turn these two areas around?

Why is that important to you?

Would you like to be known as a person of integrity and good character?

How would that feel, to have the respect of peers, parents, teachers, coaches, etc.?
There are lots of strategies and helpful hints in this workbook to get you moving towards the best you can be. But when it comes to character, it comes down to two very difficult (but freeing) things:

1 - Determine (ahead of time) that you will ALWAYS take "the high road" on every choice you are presented. Always choose the better answer or solution...

2 - Be consistent and dependable, in ALWAYS making the better decision.

Look at the two areas of your life we discussed. Analyze why you struggle in those areas. I think you will find that the starting place to make a change, is CHOOSING to make the right decision....

If you apply this (choosing to make the better choice) in all the areas of your life where you make decisions, you will begin to see an amazing pattern of success and contentment follow you! Even more importantly, you will be developing good character along the way.

AND......

Those are the people who are the leaders among us. Develop strong character!

Life Lesson #20
"Being Likeable"

"Some people are inherently likeable. If you're not – work on it. It may even improve your social life." –Antonin Scalia

#20 REVIEW:

There's just something to be said for being likable! We've all meant people who light up a room, who are surrounded by small crowds, and who make people feel good by being around them. These people aren't overinflated with their own ego or agenda. They just seem to enjoy life, and want to take you along for the ride!

Why are they like that?

Well, often they aren't wasting their time caring about what everyone is thinking about them. They know that most of the time, others are worried about "crowd thought" pertaining to **themselves**!

If you can live your life just being yourself and not be overly concerned with the opinions of others, you will find it easier to relax and truly be likeable yourself.

A few minor things you can do are: smile, be authentic & sincere, take a genuine interest in others, and laugh often! Take time to make others feel good. Compliment them. Look them in the eye when you speak to them. Think how much better of a world it would be, if we all attempted just being a little kinder to one another. Do your part, and reap the benefits of being more likable as a result.

AUTHOR COMMENT:

As I talked about in the book, one quality that I've found that many high achievers have is being likable. They know how to walk into a room and make the room light up. They are good at listening, remembering people's names, and take a real interest in others lives.

They smile, look you in the eye and aren't afraid to laugh or poke fun at **themselves**. Although it comes naturally for some, for most people... becoming likable and turning the charisma 'on', is a skill that needs to be developed.

Why is it important/beneficial to be likable? Well, whether you like it or not, you are going to have to deal with others your whole life! In the end, who you know and whether or not they find you likeable, may play a major role in your overall success.

Learning some of the little 'tricks' we've discussed here will definitely help you become better received by others in your life.

Don't take my word for it.

Try it for yourself.

I think you'll be surprised by the results!

YOUR REFLECTIONS ON LIFE LESSON #20

Think of the one person you know that seems to have "likeability" nailed down. Who is it?
What are several of the attributes they have that make them that way?

What is their best quality that draws you to them? (Sense of humor, laughter, sincerity, ability to connect with others, giving heart, kind words, etc.)

Do you possess any of that quality?

Who are some of the other people you are drawn to due to their "likeability" factor?

Name a few different attributes they possess?

PERSONAL APPLICATION

We can't be someone else, even if we admire them! You need to cultivate "likeability" qualities that fit who you are as a person, and then work on other qualities, just to be able to connect with people! These skills can be learned, but they always need to be in the context of "who you are". Authenticity and being true to yourself, are the foundation to likeability. It is just the real you, who is warmer and more open to other people...

What are your best three "likeability" qualities? (Loyalty, honesty, can keep a secrete/true friend, love to laugh, care about others and can show that, etc.)

What are 3-5 things you could be doing to make those qualities be even better?

What would be your 3 - 5 picks for "working likeability into your life", that are not your strengths right now?

Start working on those things that are strengthening the likeability qualities you already have, and then working on the others! Don't be afraid to be the best of who you are. or afraid to show that to others...

Life Lesson #21
"Being Your Best All the Time"

"No matter what the endeavor, if you don't give it your best effort, you'll never know what might have been." - Larry Fitzgerald, (football player)

LESSON #21 REVIEW:

There are going to be days when you just aren't feeling it. Your body is sore, you're sick, the weather sucks, your best friend is annoying you. You name it and it's going to happen.

However, you can't let that stop you from doing what you need to do to be great. Maybe you need to get out of bed so you can get that extra practice before school. Maybe you need to stay up a little later and study to get a good grade on the upcoming test. Maybe you have a few emails you need to send. Whatever the work is that you need to put in, get it done.

Be your best, all the time!

It's easy to do the things you need to when you feel up to it. When it's convenient, when the time is easier, when it will make you look good, etc. That's no challenge, and it won't separate you from the pack. True winners do the things that "nobody else wants to do today", so they can live tomorrow in a way that "nobody else will be able to"! Work at excelling, and be your best all the time! Why would you want to be anything less?

Refuse to be average!

AUTHOR COMMENT:

My dad always used to say, "How you do anything, is how you do everything". And to be honest, it would annoy me every time he said it!

But he was right.

How you do the little things, ends up being how you will do the big things. In all reality, the big things are just a bunch of the little things combined.

I remember I always had to do the dishes growing up. After I finished, my good ole' dad would inspect my work. I would have cleaned up a huge mess from our family dinner and occasionally he'd find an area I had overlooked. "You didn't finish the job son", he'd say. "I should be able to come in here and look around and not even be able to tell that anyone was ever in here".

Talk about attention to detail (and annoying!) But again, he was right. Why wouldn't I go the extra mile and take a few extra moments to finish the job right?

That's how we need to approach everything we do in life. Do it to the best of our ability.

Get a reputation as someone others want to work with and be around, because you do things right.

Giving your best effort all the time (especially when you don't feel like it) is a true sign of greatness.

YOUR REFLECTIONS ON LIFE LESSON #21

What are 3 activities/responsibilities you find difficult to give your best too?

Why do you think it's hard?

Will improving those areas make things better at home, at school, or with friends?

What are 3 activities/responsibilities you find easy to give your best too?

Why do you think it's easy?

Is there any part of the above that can be hard at times?

In what way?

What do you do to "push through"?

PERSONAL APPLICATION

Name 2 areas you want to challenge yourself in to do your best:

List 5 - 10 ways you can improve your success on both areas:

Jot these down and stick them on your bedroom wall, locker, or bathroom mirror. Read them every day, and work at incorporating them daily into your life!

Life Lesson #22
"Learning the Power of Forgiveness"

"To forgive is to set a prisoner free and discover that the prisoner was you." -Lewis B. Smedes

LESSON #22 REVIEW:

Before starting this lesson, I would just like to mention that I am advocating forgiveness for common wrongs many of us experience at times. If you have ever been abused, in any of its forms, you are dealing with a bigger issue than forgiveness. Please share what is happening in your life immediately with a school counselor or an adult that you trust. Don't try to carry this burden alone. We are here to help, and we care about you! -Jesse

"Holding on to bitterness is like drinking poison and expecting the other person to die." -Anonymous

Forgiveness is so powerful. Applying it can change your life radically for the better! I shared some of my own struggles with being wrongly treated in my book, and coming to terms with the power of "releasing" the anger, hurt, and frustration I was feeling. Feel free to reread that section.

Without a doubt, I'm sure awful things have been done to you as well. Unfortunately, I can pretty much promise you that unfair treatment is probably going to happen again. That's just life... However, don't let those who have wronged you, end up dictating your happiness or unhappiness. Being consumed with anger, desiring revenge, and playing over and over in your mind the injustice, allows that person to steal your joy. Now they are controlling your thoughts, your time, and your actions. No one deserves to have that kind of power over you, especially those who have wronged you. If you can "let go" of the past and forgive, it allows you to move on. Not because they deserve it... but because YOU do. Go on to live an incredible life.

Don't let bitterness rob you of your greatness!

AUTHOR COMMENT:

If there is someone in your life that you are holding bitterness against in you heart, I beg of you to forgive them.

Maybe they don't deserve it, they probably don't! However, it isn't about them, it's about YOU. I talked about how forgiving a coach changed my life. It allowed me to be happy again! It positively impacted my health, and it allowed me to see clearly... the path that I was supposes to go down in entertainment (which led to doing things that are beyond some of my wildest dreams now)!! Until I chose forgiveness, I was blinded by my hatred/hurt/frustration, and I was unable to see my true calling. How glad I am that I did! I have been able to find a fulfillment in my life that I never dreamed possible.

If there's one thing I wish for you, it's this: choose forgiveness in your life, it's a major key for success and happiness... and you deserve both!

YOUR REFLECTIONS ON LIFE LESSON #22

What is the most unfair thing that has happened to you in the past 2 years?

Where you able to straighten it out, or are you still dealing with anger or pain?

Does forgiving someone in this situation seem unfair?   Why or why not?

How do you think releasing the anger, hurt, bitterness etc. allows you to move on in a new way?

PERSONAL APPLICATION

Think of any situations where you were wronged, where you might be able to release your anger and let it go.

Try it, and see how you feel when it is no longer "playing over in your mind". You deserve to be set free and move on to be the best you can be!

SIGN & DATE:

Life Lesson #23
"Being Humble"

"Self-praise is for losers. Be a winner. Stand for something. Always have class, and be humble". -John Madden

LESSON #23 REVIEW:

"The loudest one in the room, is usually the weakest one in the room". -Anonymous

Humblness is a valuable quality, especially as you gain more success in your life. When a person gets in your face, tells you how they are the best thing going, it's a major turn off! It's cocky, insecure, and not a good look.

Don't be "that guy/gal".

If you are truly great at something, you don't need to go around shouting it out to the world. Others will find out on their own. Your bio will be much better received when it's coming from someone... who isn't you.

This can be tricky, because when you work really hard to become great at something, it feels good to be recognized. Keeping a good strong core of friends in your corner, to keep you (and your ego) in check, is a great way for you to stay on the 'humble pie' diet.

Be mindful that bragging rites are never yours,' let others do the talking for you.

Also, always sing the praises of others, and be genuinely happy for anyone else who is doing well! Wherever you are, always acknowledge the accomplishments of others, and make sure you let them feel like the star in the room.

AUTHOR NOTE:

Being humble can be hard, especially when you are a confident person. However, it is imperative that you learn to remain humble... no matter what. If you don't, you are going to rub a lot of people the wrong way. Being filled with pride is just not a healthy way to live your life.

Keep in mind, no matter how big and bad you think you are, there is always going to someone else who is bigger and "badder". Someone who has more money than you... A better car... Is better looking........... Has more fame... etc.

Instead, look for opportunities to turn pride into gratitude! Learning to embody the spirit of gratitude, caused a major turning point in my own life.

We all have so much to be thankful for. Even if it's just that we are alive, living, and breathing. That's pretty awesome! Remember this, no matter how bad you have it, there's someone out there who would kill to be in your shoes right now.

Love others. Stay humble. Work hard. Smile and be great.

YOUR REFLECTIONS ON LIFE LESSON #23

Name 2 areas you feel you have bragging rights, where it is tough to stay humble:

Are you vocal about your accomplishments, or do you let others "sing your praises"? Give an example:

How does humbleness make it easier for people to really appreciate your gift/talent/ability?

Give an example of a gifted person who is also humble:

What do you admire about them being that way?

PERSONAL APPLICATION

How amazing do you feel when others compliment you on an accomplishment (on their own)? Explain:

How do you see humbleness being a good character quality?

ADDITIONAL NOTES ON THIS LESSON:

Life Lesson #24
"Learning from Others"

"Success is no accident. It is hard work, perseverance, learning, studying, sacrifice and most of all, love of what you are doing or learning to do". -Pele (Soccer Great)

LESSON #24 REVIEW:

They say, 'some people have to learn the hard way.' Well I say, don't be one of those people! Learning the hard way is well........ hard! And it sucks. It can cost you tons of money, friendships and time.

Learning from other's successes and defeats, will get you to the top a lot faster. It can also save you a ton of heartache.

We can all be prone to stubbornness and want to do things our own way. We may think that what we are doing is 'different', that our idea is 'better', etc. The truth of the matter is this: there is nothing new under the sun. It's all been done before, and we know that history repeats itself over, and over again.

Learn to work smarter! Choose to be open, listening and learning from the experience and opinions of successful people.

In previous chapters I talked about putting yourself around people who have been successful in the arena where you want to go. Be smart. Learn from them! This is the quickest shortcut to success, and will be time well spent.

AUTHOR COMMENT:

"I never learned anything while I was talking."   -Larry King

Sometimes I haven't wanted to learn from others and I'll admit it. I can think I'm smarter, or that I will work harder than the next person, and at times that has limited my success.

Occasionally it can be good to be hard headed, but there are times when you need to put your ego aside and listen to the advice of someone with a different opinion or perspective.

Frequently, it's the thing you don't want to hear, that you <u>need</u> to hear the most.

Yeah.........OUCH!

Don't let your pride keep you from learning something valuable........something that can positively influence your life, in a major way.

This may seem like a small thing, but it can be a game changer for you. Open your eyes to learning from others. It can be a major short cut to your goal, and you should take advantage of it!

YOUR REFLECTIONS ON LIFE LESSON #24

Who are 3 of the most influential people you have learned from in your life?

Why were you drawn to them to learn, and what did they teach you?

Who are 2 additional people you would love to learn from? What would you learn?

PERSONAL APPLICATION

Make a list of several people, in your life, you would like to spend time with and learn from (a skill, a hobby, an instrument, wisdom, a sense of humor, etc.):

Make a list of several people, outside of your life; you would like to learn from (on youtube, books, magazine articles, etc.):

Begin to surround yourself with talented, smart people you can learn from!

Life Lesson #25
"Not Wasting Time on Social Media"

It takes discipline not to let social media steal your time.
-Alexis Ohanian

LESSON #25 REVIEW

Oh social media... "The dream killer". If you are reading this right now and want to be successful, be willing to give up your cell phone! That's a sad truth.

We've discussed the importance of hard work, but so many people today aren't willing to pay the price needed to be truly successful. Being busy and occupied on your feed or plugged into your phone, sucks valuable time out of your life. The funny thing is, many folks are wasting all this time watching what other people say they are doing, and half of that is all "smoke and mirrors"! To top it off, many of these people we don't even know in real life! We don't have any relationship with them. What the heck is going on?? Don't try to find validation by likes and re-tweets from strangers. Don't be one of those people; it's an unattractive quality. When you develop true confidence in yourself, you won't need to seek approval from strangers online.

Go out and live your life! Actually do something and enjoy it, without having to record every second! Live your life fully. Don't waste time and energy on trying to put up a front on social media. If you can learn to do this, it will set you head and shoulders above the pack.

AUTHOR COMMENT:

Everyone is their own 'rock star' on Facebook.

If my manager would allow me to delete my social media I would, but she is smarter than me and I have to listen to her or else I get into trouble! (Believe me, you don't want my manager mad at you!)

If there's one thing you've learned about me from my book and workbook, I bet it's this: I'm all about doing things that give me the highest shot at being successful and achieving my goals.

If that means waking up early and eating right I'm going to do it. If it means drinking lots of water and forgiving others, I'm in. Why wouldn't you want to do the things that are going to help you get to where you want to be? Take the shortcuts and use the short cuts?

I think a major problem with today's generation, is its addiction to social media. It keeps us from developing good social skills, habits, and talents (which will help us be great and stand out). Young people today aren't putting in the '10,000 hours' (the amount of time it takes to become the master of a skill) at anything. Except maybe, scrolling through photos and posts about what other people had for lunch. What a waste! Don't become a victim to this mindset, and limit your time on social media. Instead, master a craft, meet people, or learn a new language. Choose to live a life full of purpose!

YOUR REFLECTIONS ON LIFE LESSON #25

How "addicted" would you say you are to social media?   Score from 1 - 10

How much time daily, do you spend on social media, cell phones, and television?

What other activities would you like to do but don't have the time for?

Are you involved in any active activities outside the home? (Sports, music, clubs, etc.) What? How often?

PERSONAL APPLICATION

-Whatever time you recorded for amount of social media you are now on, cut that time in half over the next few weeks.

-Begin some of the activities you would like to do but don't currently have time for!

-Don't use cell phones during eating times or family time together. Get out the board games, the basketball, the bikes, anything that will get you moving and interacting with family and friends.

-Be aware of how much social media sucks up your time! Try to actually be engaged with people face to face... Give social media a rest!

ADDITIONAL NOTES ON THIS LESSON:

Life Lesson #27
"Learning to be a Giver and a Server"

The secret to living is giving.   -Tony Robbins

LESSON #27 REVIEW:

We all know that true fulfillment for living is through giving. It's about 'we' not 'me'. I invite you to explore this in your own life. Many on this planet are "Takers", thinking that is what will get them ahead in their life. Living life selfishly all the time will not bring happiness. Sadly, often the opposite happens.

What we put out into the universe comes back around.   I'm sure you've heard story after story of those who have chosen to give and serve, and have been rewarded (in many unforeseen ways), for their efforts.

However, you don't want to do good things and serve others just for the benefits you will receive... although that can be an unexpected and terrific bonus. Instead, strive to be a giver because it is the right thing to do (and it just happens to feel good to do it!). Share your blessings, and BE a blessing to others.

It's something you'll never regret.

AUTHOR COMMENT:

Some of the best moments I've experienced in my life are times when I've given back and served others. Giving is fulfilling to a degree that far exceeds anything you can do! It can also be a lot of fun!

Not all valuable giving is huge. You don't have to sell all your possessions and move to Africa to build schools. Giving can be something as simple as: dropping a quarter in someone else's expired meter, complimenting a stranger, or helping give an introduction to a person in your network that someone else could benefit from meeting.

It doesn't matter whether the act is big or small, just start serving others!

You may find (as an added bonus), that other people will want to start helping and serving you.

The whole act is contagious!

See how giving and serving others can add quality to your life. Try it, and you will also be building that strong Character we've talked about!

YOUR REFLECTIONS ON LIFE LESSON #27

What areas in your life do you volunteer, in some way to help others?

How does that make you feel?

What type of volunteering, have you seen from some of your peers?

Who do you admire that is a giver, doer, helper?

What do they do, and why do you admire them?

What are some of the needs in your school, community, family, that could use time and help from others like you?

PERSONAL APPLICATION

Name 3 places (in your community) you can think of, which would welcome you and your help:

How would you feel about being involved?
Would other family/friends want to do that with you?

Make it a habit everyday to:

-Encourage 1 person (you normally wouldn't)
-Compliment 1 person (you normally wouldn't)
-Do a kindness for 1 person (you normally wouldn't)
-Smile & show kindness to 1 person who you often see but don't speak to: school secretary, janitor, etc.

After 1 week of doing the above, write a small paragraph on how it feels to reach out beyond your circle of friends"

Life Lesson #15
"Believing that Anything is Possible"

"What is the difference between an obstacle and an opportunity? Our attitude toward it. Every opportunity has a difficulty, and every difficulty has an opportunity." -J. Sidlow Baxter

LESSON #15 REVIEW:

What you think, you are.

One thing I've noticed about highly successful people is, despite the odds (or even if the odds aren't in their favor) they tend to have a sort of supreme confidence in themselves and their vision.

You see this in interviews after players win the Superbowl, or other big championships. They look dead into the camera and say, "I knew I was the best and I'd be here someday." Although it can seem a little cocky, there is something to be said about a person who passionately believes in themselves, their dream, and their pursuit to be the best they can.

Of course there are a lot of other important factors that have to happen: hard work, hustle, right time right place, etc. etc., but it all starts with your thoughts!

Believe in yourself!
Believe in your dream!
If you can think it, you can achieve it.

AUTHOR COMMENT:

A quote I often use in my speeches is, "One man thought he could, the other man thought he couldn't. They both were right."

There is so much power in the thoughts you play over and over again in your own mind. This can be a good thing (positive thoughts, believing in yourself), or a bad thing (negative, doubting, thoughts).

The key is to work hard at what you want in this life, believe in yourself, value your efforts, and aspire to all that you are capable of.

You can accomplish a lot more than you think! But you have to believe in yourself, and believe that anything is possible.

Choose to believe in yourself.

Choose to believe that anything is possible.

There will be no telling what you can achieve!

YOUR REFLECTIONS ON LIFE LESSON #15

What is an example of something in the past you thought was impossible for you to learn or master, that you now can do?

What made it seem impossible?

How were you able to make it possible? What changed?

What do you feel is impossible for you today?

PERSONAL APPLICATION

Select that one thing that has seemed out of your reach, and determine to do everything you can to conquer it! Take action, write goals, work hard, learn from others, whatever it takes............ you are capable of so much more than you think!

Reread the important parts of my book. Encourage yourself with the steps in the workbook, which will point you towards success. There is a fantastic life out there just for you, but you will have to run & work towards it!

ADDITIONAL NOTES ON THIS LESSON:

Life Lesson #1
"Work on Tweaking Your Dream"

"Things are only impossible until they're not". ~Jean-Luc Picard, Star Trek: The Next Generation

LESSON #1 REVIEW:

Part of my dream was realized with hard work over many years time, I did get that full ride scholarship to college! Yet, as college graduation neared, I had to begin investigating other ways (than the NBA) to continue to play basketball and make a living at it. I had to deal with fear, insecurity, and dwindling funds. My path went a lot of directions, but I kept learning as I went and tried to "stumble forward" at times, in the direction of my dreams.

AUTHOR COMMENT:

I always wanted to be an NBA player. I wanted to get PAID to play basketball! That was my biggest dream and I went for it 100%. At a certain point it became clear that it just wasn't going to happen for me and I won't lie, that realization was hard to stomach. But I stayed open to 'tweaking' my dream. I knew what I really loved..... the game of basketball, competing, and connecting with people who were as passionate about the game as I was.

Once I allowed myself to be open to 'tweaking' (or adjusting my dream), I realized that there were a lot of other things I could do that centered around my passion for the game. I could be a coach, referee, trainer, commentator, or work with all kinds of groups like the Boys and Girls club etc.

Eventually, by pursuing basketball commercials, I was able to "tweak" my newly found abilities into my current job......... a basketball entertainer, actor, author and youth speaker. The satisfaction I now receive from doing all of these things, has given me a life more fulfilling then playing in the NBA! Not a bad adjustment to a dream millions of kids start out with!

Start thinking outside the box, what are some new ways you could make a living doing what you love that you might not have thought of before?

You may have a passion that has nothing to do with sports, but all of these Life Lessons still can work for you. If you are jazzed by music, art, culinary studies, dog training, game inventing, or a million other things, you can look at your passion from new angles and with new eyes.........and find amazing opportunities you never knew existed.

Sometimes we just "don't know, what we don't know", until we push ourselves to learn it. Your dreams and passions are worth the effort!

YOUR REFLECTIONS ON LIFE LESSON #1:

-In what way can you personally relate to my struggles?

-In what way are your struggles different?

-What new possibilities do you see that you didn't before?

PERONAL APPLICATION:

1) List 3-5 possible ways you could use your dream or passion in life to make a living that you hadn't considered:

2) List 3-5 avenues to investigate which might give you leads on possibilities you hadn't considered in your field (talking/emailing someone in the industry, goggling your area of interest, volunteering for an organization that is involved with your focus area, etc.):

*Remember, this is an ongoing exercise. Be observant and always watching and listening for new ways to market and brand yourself. Jot those ideas down when you get them, and investigate new ways to make those idea's happen.

ADDITIONAL NOTES ON THIS LESSON:

Life Lesson #28
"Having a Great Attitude"

"Things work out best for those who make the best of the way things work out." -John Wooden

LESSON #28 REVIEW/and FINAL THOUGHTS

You are going to have two choices over and over again in your life.

You can get bitter or you can get better.

Don't get bitter, make excuses, blame other people and give up with out trying. That's a victim's mentality.

That's how unsuccessful people think.
That's the easy way out and it takes no guts.

What you decide in these moments will dictate where you ultimately end up in your life. I hope you choose to get better.

I want you <u>to get better</u>. Take 100% responsibility for your life. Throw away those excuses and create the dream life you deserve to live. I really hope you'll become the <u>master of your attitude.</u> The sooner you can learn this, the better.

Bad things are going to happen to all of us, I don't want to sound negative but it's the truth. You can choose to be a victim or you can choose to <u>rise above your circumstances</u> and create the life you want to live. The choice is totally up to you.

Always choose wisely.

Take the "high road" when you make every decision. We can all make a million excuses for why we make a poor decision, but we all instinctively know what the "higher road" decision should be.

Remember, you only have one life. You should do everything you can to live it fully, <u>with a big heart for others</u>, and with total joy!

AUTHOR COMMENT:

If there is one thing I can say with certainty it's this: your own attitude, is what will determine if you are successful or not in life.

If you take away one thing from my speeches, my book, or my workbook...take away this:

The biggest obstacle you will ever have to overcome is yourself.

It doesn't matter what other people say or think, the only thing that matters is what you think.

Your own attitude will dictate if you will be a winner or loser in life, and the greatest thing about attitude is this: **you** get to choose what it will be every day; **you** get to pick how you will respond to every situation.

No one gets to do it **but you.**

Not your teachers, your coaches, your parents, your friends, your siblings.

Your own attitude is the one thing in life that only you can control.

If you can learn to be the master of your own attitude, I can promise you will live a happier and more successful life. I may not know a lot, but if there is one thing I know beyond the shadow of a doubt........ it's these 3 words:

ATTITUDE IS EVERYTHING!

CHOOSE EVERYDAY, WITH EVERY DECISION, TO BE THE MASTER OF YOUR OWN ATTITUDE! THERE IS NO OTHER POSITION YOU CAN TAKE, THAT GIVES YOU THE POWER TO ACT, REACT, AND MOVE FORWARD, AS COURAGEOUSLY AS MAKING THE CHOICE TO HAVE A GOOD ATTITUDE!

APPENDIX A - Follow-up Reflections

What has changed, in your thinking, at: 3 Months into using the principles outlined:

DATE:

-Do you see a problem as a set back, or is it an opportunity? Why? How? Explain.

-Do situations control how you react, or do you choose your own responses to any situation? Give 2 examples:

1)

2)

-Do you respect others? How? What does that look like?

-Do you respectfully stand up for yourself and teach others how to treat you? What does that "look" like?

-Do you notice and engage with the people around you that others "don't see"? (The custodian at school, the kid who has a hard time fitting in, the cashier at the market, the neighbor that suffers from Alzheimer's etc.) Give 2 examples:

1)

2)

-Does your economic/social/racial (etc.) background act as a stumbling block or excuse for you to NOT move forward, or do you take complete responsibility for your life and the future you can carve for yourself---- despite those issues? What's changed in your thinking?

6 Months into using the principles outlined:

DATE:

-Do you see a problem as a set back, or is it an opportunity? Why? How? Explain.

-Do situations control how you react, or do you choose your own responses to any situation? Give 2 examples:

1)

2)

-Do you respect others? How? What does that look like?

-Do you respectfully stand up for yourself and teach others how to treat you? What does that "look" like?

-Do you notice and engage with the people around you that others "don't see"? (The custodian at school, the kid who has a hard time fitting in, the cashier at the market, the neighbor that suffers from Alzheimer's etc.) Give 2 examples:

1)

2)

-Does your economic/social/racial (etc.) background act as a stumbling block or excuse for you to NOT move forward, or do you take complete responsibility for your life and the future you can carve for yourself---- despite those issues? What's changed in your thinking?

<u>9 Months</u> into using the principles outlined:

DATE:

-Do you see a problem as a set back, or is it an opportunity? Why? How? Explain.

-Do situations control how you react, or do you choose your own responses to any situation? Give 2 examples:

1)

2)

-Do you respect others? How? What does that look like?

-Do you respectfully stand up for yourself and teach others how to treat you? What does that "look" like?

-Do you notice and engage with the people around you that others "don't see"? (The custodian at school, the kid who has a hard time fitting in, the cashier at the market, the neighbor that suffers from Alzheimer's etc.) Give 2 examples:

1)

2)

-Does your economic/social/racial (etc.)
background act as a stumbling block or excuse for
you to NOT move forward, or do you take complete
responsibility for your life and the future you can
carve for yourself---- despite those issues?

What has changed in your thinking?

FINALLY:

What do your answers (over the past 9 months) tell you about how you've moved forward in:

-Your commitment to your dream?

-Changing your attitude & how you think about success?

-Whether or not you feel stronger, more motivated, or closer to determining your future?

ADDITIONAL NOTES TO YOURSELF:

Made in the USA
San Bernardino, CA
12 April 2018